Matt
296 7495 h
238 1050 w
Botchery

Riddle Me This

Riddle Me This

A World Treasury
of Word Puzzles,
Folk Wisdom, and
Literary Conundrums

PHIL COUSINEAU

CONARI PRESS
Berkeley, California

Conari Press books are distributed by Publishers Group West.

Cover and book design by Claudia Smelser

Library of Congress Cataloging-in-Publication Data

Cousineau, Phil.
   Riddle me this : a world treasury of word puzzles, folk wisdom, and literary conundrums / Phil Cousineau.
       p.   cm.
   Includes bibliographical references (p. 166–175).
   ISBN: 1-57324-145-8
   1. Riddles.   I. Title
PN6371.C68
398.6—dc21   98–54332
                                                                  CIP

Printed in the United States of America on recycled paper
99 00 01 02 03 RRD(H) 10 9 8 7 6 5 4 3 2 1

For the enigmatic
James Van Harper
who has riddled our lives
with humor

Is the wit quicke?
Then do not sticke
To read these riddles darke:
Which if thou doe,
And rightly too,
Thou art a witty sparke.

—*Title page from* The Booke of Meery Riddles, *1629*

Tell all the truth,
But tell it slant.

—*Emily Dickinson*

All true wisdom comes in the form of a riddle.

—*Henry Miller*

Riddle Me This

Foreword   ix

I   The Introductory   1

II   The Pleasury   31

III   The Guessery   141

IV   The Sourcery   165

V   The Unforgettery   179

Foreword

There is an essential riddle that each of us must confront at some moment in our lives. It has to do with who we are and why we are here—the meaning of life. This riddle is handed out to everyone who is born a human being.

All of the riddles in this wondrous book dance around that central riddle. As we read each one, we enter a familiar place of the unknown, where the mind hits the edge of reason and stops for a moment. But we maintain the conviction that with enough twisting of brain and wrinkling of brow, we just might come to the answer. So we turn the enigma over and over in our mind, looking for the trick entrance, the clue that alters our perspective in such a way that we can finally see into the knot of the thing. Success brings a rush of joy. We have proved that we are clever enough at least to figure out some things in life.

This book is a great delight, and not only when I am able to solve a riddle. As I read the riddles themselves—coming from many cultures and historical eras—I feel as though I am looking into the trickster side of the mind of all the world's peoples, seeing into our common questions, and into our bemusement with our own wily nature. If you keep this book around for awhile, it will serve you well. For one thing, a good riddle to solve every day will keep your mind occupied and free it from worrying about the truly trivial things in life. I personally am working through the riddles in the book from beginning to end. I expect that once my mind gets really good at solving them, it will then be sharp enough to take on the central riddle. Once I master that, then I presume I will win the hand of the fairest in the land, get the gold, the kingdom, and live happily ever after. Isn't that how it works? Good luck to one and all.

Wes "Scoop" Nisker
author of *Crazy Wisdom*

The Introductory

What is it that
walks with four legs in the morning,
with two legs at midday, and with three legs
when the sun has gone down?

Should you be wily enough to answer this curious question correctly, as Oedipus did when he was challenged by a strange creature on the road to ancient Thebes, you too will have solved one of the most confounding problems ever to face a wayward traveler. Dispatched by the gods to prevent travelers from reaching the city, the fabulous beast had perched herself on a cliff outside the city, and seized all who tried to pass by. Those who couldn't think quickly—or imaginatively—enough she hurled to their deaths, or devoured.

But Oedipus outwitted her.

"It is *a human being*," he answered calmly, "who crawls on all fours as a baby, walks upright on two legs in middle age, and in old age stumbles along with a cane."

The writers of old said the creature was so shamed by Oedipus' clever deduction that she hurled herself off the precipice. Who was this menacing creature, and what about her has haunted the world's imagination ever since? And what does her dramatic confrontation say about the enigmatic powers of the human imagination?

> I am older than the pyramids.
> I am the daughter of Titans.
> I have the body of a lion, the wings of a bird,
> and the head and breasts of a woman.
> I am more obscure than oracles,
> and more puzzling than gods.
> I ask travelers questions that their lives depend on.
> *O wise one, weigh your words well and say what I am.*

If you answered, *the Sphinx*, you have identified a character who has tantalized commentators for centuries, and you have begun to crack the mystery of the imagination. Many people have regarded the Sphinx's treatment of unfortunate wayfarers as merely the vengeance of the gods. But there is more than one way to read myths, which are sacred precisely because they reflect inexhaustible mysteries. Myth's power to stir the soul depends on each generation breathing new life into them, as the Egyptians did with the story of the Sphinx, which was already ancient when they immortalized her in stone along the banks of the Nile.

Forty centuries later, the monument still stares out at us over the desert sands, and her name is remembered for her challenges to travelers and for her time-devouring gaze that questions everything from here to eternity.

THE MOTHER WIT

I am as enchanting as a medieval spell,
charming as a nursery rhyme, as challenging as a duel.
I accompany you from cradle to grave,
providing laughter for childhood,
literary games for middle age,
and wisdom tests for elders.
Guess my gnomic name, if you can.

Walk around these words I have cobbled together as you would walk around the sands that surround the Sphinx. Take a leap of imagination. Tease the answer out of its hiding place. Turn these words around like a whetstone in your mind, then turn to these, "When first I appear I seem mysterious, but when I am explained I am nothing serious." Sharpen your wit on these old English words; hone your sense of humor on them, and soon the playful subject of this book will be revealed to you as the noble *riddle*.

Described variously as enigmas, conundrums, puzzle poems, bafflers, charades, logogriphs, teasers, verbal jigsaws, queer words, and quiz questions, since olden times riddles have been posed to test people's wit and stretch their imaginations. Riddles reveal the prodigious imagination of our ancestors and throughout history have given a voice to those who were not commonly heard.

According to Webster's, a riddle is "a proposition put in obscure or ambiguous terms to puzzle or exercise the ingenuity in discovering its meaning; something to be solved by conjecture." The Dutch folklorist Jan Van Hunyard has written, "Folk riddles are traditional questions with unexpected answers, verbal puzzles that circulate, mostly by word of mouth, to demonstrate the cleverness of the questioner and challenge the wit of his audience." For French anthropologist Claude Lévi-Strauss, a riddle was "an overt question with a covert answer." My own favorite description is given by an old African American story-teller from the South, who drawled, "A riddle is what you guess up on."

In the spirit of conciseness, we can hazard a guess, so to speak, that riddles are simply *ingenious questions in search of clever answers:*

> Guess a riddle now you must:
> Stone is fire, and fire is dust,
> Black is red, and red is white—
> Come and view the wondrous sight.

In other words, the genius of the Sphinx is in the way her question allows us to see the "lie that tells the truth," as Picasso once described the beauty of art, and as the traditional riddle from England just quoted tells us about *coal.* Consider also this old Turkish riddle: "It enters the forest and does not rustle" and its unexpected answer, *the shadow.* And this Spanish one: "A lazy old woman has a tooth in her crown, and with that tooth she gathers the people," with its clanging answer, *a bell.*

At first glance or hearing, a riddle may seem to be incomprehensible, but perhaps a more fruitful descriptor would be *enigmatic* (literally "a dark saying"); the solving of a riddle can bring light to the imagination. Part of the genius of riddles is the way they illustrate the perennial wisdom that things aren't always what they seem, and the manner in which they reveal the "genius," the vital life, in everything.

For at least six thousand years, the riddle was held in high esteem. But in modern times, it has unfortunately been relegated to the playgrounds of children and delegated to the research projects of folklorists. Unless disguised in the form of a detective story or mathematical mind-cruncher, for most modern adults riddles are, frankly, exasperating. The most honor the word *riddle* receives today is when it is used to express a respectably mysterious problem: "The Olmec Riddle," or "The Riddle of Time." However, a closer look reveals that riddles—true riddles—rank alongside myths, legends, fairy tales, maxims, and proverbs, as one of the earliest types of folk wisdom. From Borneo longhouses to Comanche tepees, from Anglo-Saxon mead halls to the huts of Laplander nomads, riddles have flourished as a way to pass the time—or question it. An even deeper look reveals that riddles were a favorite form of wordplay and brain teaser for many of the greatest minds in history, from Aristotle to Emily Dickinson, Leonardo da Vinci to James Joyce.

The source of riddles' charm remains similar from culture to culture, era to era. It begins at the beginning, with lullabies: "Twinkle, twinkle little star / How I wonder what you are. . . ." My grandfather, Sydney England, my mother has long been fond of telling me, used to lull her to sleep each evening with a different set of riddles, ending with these lilting words: "Riddle, riddle, where are you? Riddle, riddle, I love you. . . ."

Riddles thrive not only on wonder, but on sheer surprise. Imagine this one, if you will: "This girl, who has six legs and two arms, often prepares to go on a journey. She starts out with a bang, but still rocks ever pitching [like a ship] in the same place."

Our lives are literally riddled from the *cradle* (the answer to the Icelandic riddle quoted earlier), to the *grave* (the answer to this African one): "My house has no lamp." No wonder riddles have been called "the mother wit." They give birth to the child called "poetry," and the grandchild named "joy."

TO PROVE WITH HARD QUESTIONS

He happened to be the only child,
But his father and mother are not known.

In this example from the Philippines, *the riddle* is the only child of unknown parents. She is a linguistic orphan, but her heritage can be discovered in the roots of her name. *Riddle* derives from the Old English word *raedal,* meaning "to give advice," and also shares the same root as the verb *to read.* Its secondary meaning, "a coarse-meshed sieve," has its origins in the Old English *hriddel,* "to sift," but is not unconnected. Uncannily, the riddle allows us to sift through false meanings looking for true ones. We also speak of being "riddled with doubt," suggesting we have "holes" in our convictions. In other words, we don't have all the answers.

In the proverbial nutshell, traditional folk riddles are quizzical questions with anonymous authors. The footprints of the oldest ones, such as the enigma of the Sphinx, have disappeared underneath the tides of time. We only know that they have been passed down for generations by word of mouth from the peasants and sages of every culture. Brahmen priests propounded riddles in the sacred pages of the *Rig Veda,*

Mohammed posed them in the *Koran.* In the Old Testament, Josephus tells of the King of Tyre, Hiram, and wise Solomon, waging a riddle contest. In Kings I, when the Queen of Sheba "heard of the fame of Solomon...she came to prove him with hard questions." In other words, to test his legendary wisdom. The Hebrew warrior Samson is chronicled in Judges 14 as staging a riddle party for the thirty Philistine guests, and posing this inscrutable riddle: "Out of eater came forth meat, and out of the strong came forth sweetness." The hero's opponents tricked the answer out of his bride: *He ate honey out of a honeycomb in the carcass of a lion he had recently killed.* The folklorist Charles Potter describes this challenge as a *riddle strife,* "one of those exciting tournaments of wit held in ancient times when men might bet their fortunes, wives, daughters, and even their lives on their cleverness in riddle guessing."

Eventually riddles were transcribed into many cultures' sacred texts, then into compilations for popular entertainment. The oldest collection is found in eighth-century Anglo-Saxon poetry. *The Exeter Book,* which contains ninety-five riddles, with poetry that still casts a spell, on subjects such as snow and swords. Later collections include a book of riddles called *Amusing Questions,* published in 1511 by a printer named Wynkyn de Worde. But listen closely: If his name is pronounced quickly—"winking of word"—you can hear a mellifluous metaphor for the riddle! Is the author telling us under an assumed name that riddles are a "winking of words"? Other collections include books with equally melodious titles such as *Gnomologia* and *Aenigmata,* which were among the first printed books. Riddles appear in the *The Arabian Nights Entertainments, The Grimm Brothers Fairy Tales, The Mother Goose Rhymes,* and in J. R. R. Tolkien's *The Lord of the Rings.* Robert Graves described in *The White Goddess* how arcane religious secrets in ancient Britain were hidden in challenging riddles. Riddles appear in rituals, such as Druid initiations, African birth ceremonies, Filipino harvest festivals, and the Hawaiian *hoopaapaa* riddling contests designed to discover the worthiest of the chief's sons.

The riddlic tradition continued throughout the Renaissance. Leonardo da Vinci practiced drawing rebuses (pictorial riddles) and a series of "riddle songs," which were wordplays on the sounds of the names of musical notes. Shakespeare himself was fond of riddles. In *A Midsummer's Night's Dream,* Lysander "riddles very prettily," and Berowne describes love as "subtle as a riddle." Goethe, Swift, Cervantes, Coleridge, Austen, and Blake all practiced the perplexing art. The composers Puccini,

Elgar, and Grieg wrote opera plots that hinged on riddles. In her poetry and letters, Emily Dickinson often used riddles to describe matters too subtle or forbidden during her time to be written any other way. Literary critics have described James Joyce's labyrinthine novel, *Finnegans Wake,* as one enormous riddle. The metaphor makes an appearance on the basketball court when Zen master-basketball coach Phil Jackson writes in *Sacred Hoops,* that "each game is a riddle that must be solved, and there are no textbook answers."

THE WHETSTONE OF WORDS

What goes round and round and round,
but never gets anywhere?

"It is an excellent practice to rede riddles," reads an eleventh-century Anglo-Saxon text. Illustrative of this belief is a nineteenth-century collection of riddles that was published under the title, "A Whetstone for Dull Wits," suggesting that riddles may sharpen our wits, as the above riddle for *whetstone* demonstrates.

To many cultures, the ritual of romantic courting entailed serious riddling contests. In 1783, Christfrid Ganander wrote of the tradition of the Old Goths, "Our ancestors in this kingdom tested with riddles the acuity, intelligence and skills of each other. . . . Also when a suitor or a young man came to ask for a girl, three or more riddles were posed to him, to test his mind with them, and if he could answer and interpret them, he received the girl, otherwise not, but was classified as stupid and good for nothing. . . . Lastly, one takes note that the young folks, boys and girls, test each other still at present with riddles in our province; it is shameful if the other cannot answer three riddles, and they then send [her] to the yard of shame. . . . "

Until the nineteenth century, old men in Brittany were still ritualistically asking each other riddles in the cemetery after funeral banquets. "Riddling past the graveyard," you might say. As one commentator has written, during wakes in the Aru archipelago, while the corpse is being "uncoffined" or shown for mourning purposes, the deceased's survivors "propound riddles to each other." For tribes such as the Igorots of northern Luzon in the Philippines, the riddling that takes place during wakes is prearranged by the hosts, who partake in riddling, poetry, and cards "to get away from the drowsiness or sleepiness likely to overcome guests" and "kill the monotony of a night."

According to Charles Potter, cracking tough riddles at a ritual gathering may involve sympathetic magic thinking. For example, a wedding riddle may encourage a young couple to think they might similarly tackle and find the solution for many of the vexed problems of married life. "At any rate," writes Potter, "it would start them off in the atmosphere of accomplishment and the aura of success. For the hidden belief is that *solving a riddle may help answer an enigma in one's life.*" True folk riddles possess quicksilver flashes of an ancient way of observing the world, and remind us of why riddles have long been "used by kings, judges, oracles, and others to test a person's wisdom or worthiness."

Potter recollects the childhood riddling sessions with his parents, which were, "mind-stretching, for the answer to each new riddle was not given to me until I had tried long and hard and turned the given situation every which way seeking the solution." Often, families cracked nuts while they tried to figure out the riddles, hence the origin of the term "cracking riddles." Catharine Ann McCollum writes in "Winter Evenings in Iowa" that pioneer families used to pose riddles to one another while carpet rags were being sewn and mended, and while the family did other work.

So much a part of life were riddles, according to Potter, that through the turn of the century most young children in the American South would have giggled at the obviousness of the following riddle:

> I have an apple I can't cut,
> A blanket I can't fold,
> And so much money I can't count it.

The children would have been able to accomplish wonderful associative leaps to figure out the answer—*Sun, sky, and stars* (round apple, round sun; the blanketed sky; the richness of a sky full of stars)—because riddles had been passed down for generations, and it was customary to look and observe the ordinary world for correspondences and analogies, the "genius" of riddles.

> Little Nancy Etticoat, in a white petticoat,
>   and a red nose.
> The longer she stands, the shorter she grows.

This traditional puzzler about *a glowing candle* demonstrates more than any theory how riddling combines beauty, mystery, and logic. Archer Taylor, the brilliant folklorist and world authority on riddles, believed that descriptive riddles such as this traditional English one, "describe objects in intentionally misleading terms—we can call it metaphor or group-language, if we like—and deal with externalities of the object. Humpty Dumpty tells of a man who rolls, falls, and is injured beyond being put together again. Little Nancy Etticoat describes a candle as a girl who becomes shorter the longer she lives. These descriptions are true enough but have nothing to do with the uses of an egg or candle. A child of ten or eleven years sees objects in this way and enjoys and remembers them. An adult no longer sees them in this way and no longer remembers riddles."

THE GUESSERY

What is that which has never been felt,
Never been seen, never been heard,
Never existed,
And still has a name?

Why is figuring out a riddle like this such a "hard nut to crack" for us today? Have we thrown so much into our "forgettery" (as

Carl Sandburg described the place where we should toss all the things that are crowding our memory) that we have lost touch with our natural talent for poetry? Was there ever a time when it was considered desirable to solve deliciously difficult word games?

During Anglo-Saxon times, *riddle strifes* were held in the mead halls after great battles. A "gleeman" challenged the warriors with epic riddles and the hall reverberated with the bawdy shouts of warriors trying to solve them. This was considered so difficult it was believed that there must be a special place in the brain just for solving riddles. That place was dubbed the "guessery," the place in your mind where you have been frantically pacing (or leaping ahead to the end of this paragraph) to come up with the solution for the preceding riddle, which is—*a secret.*

Over time, the practice of turning language upside down and inside out metamorphosed into several other forms, the names of which are often used interchangeably. However, there are some useful distinctions:

❦ The *catch* riddle is more joke than riddle. It is the most commonly heard riddle today, heard on children's playgrounds and read in bathroom humor books. "How did the sheriff find the missing barber?" *He combed the town.* "How can you climb Mount Everest without getting pooped?" *By being born on top.*

🐾 The *conundrum* is a riddle whose solution relies on puns. "When is a door not a door? *When it's a jar.* "What mysterious object did the cook see in the frying pan?" *An unidentified frying object.* "When was baseball first mentioned in the Bible?" *In the big inning (beginning).*

🐾 The *puzzle* or *problem question* requires a single solution: "A Boy Scout climbed a tall pine tree to gather some acorns. He tried all morning, but couldn't get any. Why not?" *Because acorns don't grow on pine trees. They grow on oak trees.*

🐾 The *nonrational riddle* or *koan* is "spiritually instructive," in the memorable phrase of Jon Winokur, and presented from a master to students in order to compel them "beyond logic to sudden illumination." Traditional Eastern koans include the familiar "What is the sound of one hand clapping?" Or, "What is the way?" a monk asked Master Haryo, who replied, "An open-eyed man falling into the well." A Western version would be Bertoldt Brecht's stumper, "What happens to the hole when the cheese is gone?" Or Satchel Paige's "How old would you be if you didn't know how old you were?" Or Gertrude Stein's last words, "But what is the question?"

❦ The *nonverbal riddle, the droodle* or *rebus:*

> YYUR
> YYUB
> ICUR
> YY4me

which means: *Too wise you are / Too wise you be / I see you are / Too wise for me.*

❦ The *true riddle* works with associations, pretending to be one thing while being another; comparisons between something in the question and the unstated answer; or unexpected resemblances, such as playful or sexual innuendo.

> On yonder hill there is a red deer:
> The more you shoot, the more you may,
> You cannot drive that deer away.

If there is a "key" that will unlock the safe of riddle solutions, it is this time-tested combination of delightful deception and fanciful description. Phrased as a question, the example is a riddle. Turned around, it is metaphorical: "The red deer is rising over the hill" is poetic shorthand. Both forms allow us to see *the sun* in a fresh way, if we use our "guessery" correctly, and to enjoy the metamorphosis, the sudden change in meaning that words take on.

Twenty-five centuries ago, Aristotle unraveled the mystery of how metaphors and riddles imply one another. "Astonishment is and was from the beginning what led men to philosophize; they felt a yearning to the solution of riddles."

He went on to write in his *Rhetoric:*

> While metaphor is a very frequent instrument of clever sayings, another or an additional instrument is deception, as people are more clearly conscious of having learned something from their sense of surprise at the way in which a sentence ends and their soul seems to say, "Quite true and I had missed the point." This, too, is the result of pleasure afforded by clever riddles; they are instructive and metaphorical in their expression.

There are few people as adept at this blend of pleasure, instruction, and metaphor as the Irish, as displayed in this fine riddle: "It's a very big house, it's a candlestick of gold, it's a speckled robe. Measure it quickly, or spread it yonder."

Seeing and speaking of *the heavens* like this brings a thrill of recognition, and reminds us of the transformative power of words. Rediscovering a simple *oyster,* as in this old Chinese riddle, "'Twixt two curved tiles he makes his home; I'm sure from there he'll never roam," helps us realize once more the beauty of the ordinary.

"Marvel on marvel, six legs and four ears," goes the French riddle about *a man and his horse.*

And we do marvel, if we can, so we can see, once more.

THE QUIZZICAL ART

"Well, I want to know if you can tell me who are the parties that never get tired of motioning to come?"

Riddles, such as the one from the Arapaho Indians on *the eyelids,* may frustrate at first, but ultimately they delight, with their revelation of resemblances, their search for the poetry in the ordinary. They dare us to tease apart the meaning of words set to unfamiliar music.

Questions, puzzles, and challenges are at the heart of our subject. During the Middle Ages, riddling games began with three questions: "*Quis? Quae? Quid?*" ("Who, what, where?"). Eventually, *Quis,* the first of the Latin words, metamorphosed into our English "quiz," the word we use to question, interrogate, challenge. Much of our sacred teaching takes this form, from parable to drama. King Lear asks, "Who is it that can tell me who I am?" Dame Ragnall asks Sir Gawain, "What is it that a woman wants?" And the answers to these eternal questions unfold through the story.

Traditional openings in English include: "Riddle me, riddle me ree," or, "Now guess this one" and "Guess what it is." In Turkey, the phrase, "Guess it!" is a popular beginner. In Spanish you can hear, "Guess, Mr. Guesser!" In the American South, players shout out, "Let's play riddles" and "Can you guess one up?" Among the Kamba in Africa, the sessions begin with "Catch this riddle," while the Zezuru people say, "Let us swap riddles," and the Kalanga challenge each other with variations of "Let us puzzle one another" such as: "I puzzle you with a melon that fell among the pumpkins."

All these forms are rhapsodies on the theme of what I like to think of as *mischievous testing*. Archer Taylor concluded that a riddle is "one which compares an object to another entirely different object." In the Kalanga poser, a melon and pumpkins are compared to "the moon among the stars." In the Gypsy riddle, "It runs and runs and yet does not run away, it longs for sunlight and yet never sees it," *the heart* is cleverly compared first to perhaps a clock, then something vaguely human that can actually feel longing. The heart and a clock are "entirely different," as Taylor suggests, but, in the uncanny world of riddles, they *resemble* each other. "It" runs, but doesn't, longs for sun, but can't see.

The Mbeere tribe in Africa even have a one-word riddle that reveals one of the myriad secrets of the ancient form: "Resemblances." The laconic answer: *Twins.*

In the poetic and musical world of folk riddles, everything has its "twin" in the world; everything can be described in terms of something else.

Guess up, guess on, guess this. Riddle me this, riddle me on, and expound my riddle rightly. . . .

THE TREASURY

It takes more than one to say a riddle.

—*Dusun saying, North Borneo*

In the inaugural issue of *Journal of American Folklore,* in April 1888, the editors wrote that they were proposing to create a society "For the collection of the fast-vanishing remains of Folk-lore in America. . . ."

Riddle Me This is a treasury of imagination-stretching questions, puzzles, and challenges from around the world in which this particular kind of folklore is still "fast-vanishing." I believe wholeheartedly in the notion that our knowledge of the universe is threaded together by human conversation. But I also realize we live in a time marked by a rapid loss of the traditional forms of communication. While there has been a revival of storytelling and a profusion of proverb collections, there are few contemporary collections of riddles, and none that attempt even a modest sampling from around the world.

That notable first issue of *Journal of American Folklore* also announced that folklore needed to be collected because "a great change" was about to overtake the world of traditional people, mainly the Indian tribes, and the collection "must be done quickly." I have the feeling that *not* appreciating the ancient riddling game reveals a "diminished imagination," while practicing it can be useful, entertaining, and even edifying.

Riddle Me This is a cross-cultural anthology that ranges around the world. My selections are those of an unabashed dilettante, literally "one who takes delight" in wordplay and an "enigmatologist" in the spirit of Charles Potter, who concluded, "I am beginning to suspect that a riddle, a real folk riddle, represents a group effort of some humble but intelligent people to find or create a little humor or beauty or both in the rather bleak and often difficult world in which they find themselves . . . at every problem from all sides, and still keep a sense of humor."

This book is organized into sections: "The Pleasury," my revival of another marvelous old collective noun, which houses the riddles themselves, and lists the cultures from which I have best been able to determine they originate. The selections are not organized by country or theme, for this would give too many hints to the solution of the riddles and would take away much of the pleasure that they afford. Instead the riddles are loosely organized by a kind of musical theme that will soon be noticed by the avid reader. This format offers the chance for "startling juxtapositions" that honor the "rich and paradoxical nature" of riddles.

The solutions to the riddles dwell in the next section, "The Guessery," in honor of those word-warriors whose sat for hours on their mead-benches rummaging through their memory. In the spirit of poet Emily Dickinson, who wrote to her sister-in-law, "In a Life that stopped guessing you and I would not feel at home," I strongly suggest that the reader resist the temptation to seek the solutions too quickly. Instead, try to prolong the "pleasury" as long as possible by hazarding, venturing, or risking as many guesses as possible to the riddles. The third section, "The Sourcery," refers to the source material, the books and journals from which the riddles in this book were selected.

So *Riddle Me This* is more than a collection of diversions; it's a clarion call for more wordplay among us all, as witnessed, crafted, and exercised in the "peripatetic, poetic and sweet" language of riddles. It is a reminder that it is indeed an excellent practice to *rede riddles,* if only to keep our wits about us. If we do, perhaps we can find a place for them in our everyday lives, but that will happen only if we actually use them. A few lines from the Book of Proverbs suggest why riddles might be valuable:

> To give prudence to the simple,
> to the young knowledge and discretion;
> That the wise man may hear, and increase in learning,
> and the man of understanding may attain unto wise
>   counsels;
> To understand a proverb and a figure,
> the words of the wise and their dark sayings [enigmas].

In practice, you may find that reading and reciting riddles

to children during during your time together bring a degree of glee to their faces. "A riddle, a riddle, I suppose, a thousand eyes, and never a nose." *A potato.*

"If you woke up at night and scratched your head, what time would it be?" *Five to one.* "What goes ninety-nine clump?" *A caterpillar with a stump.* "It has a head like a cat, feet like a cat, a tail like a cat, but it isn't a cat." *A kitten.* "What goes up the chimney down—or down the chimney down, but never up the chimney up—or down the chimney up?" *An umbrella.*

You may add some flair to your next company meeting about employee relations by beginning it with a specially chosen riddle from Barbados about *an equal:*

> What God never sees;
> What the king seldom sees;
> What we see every day;
> Read my riddle, I pray.

If you are a teacher, try opening your next lecture or presentation with an enigmatic description about *the memory and the mind,* such as this one from the Philippines:

> The head is its residence.
> It is possessed by all.

It is with you, it is with me.
It flies without wings.

As Aristotle concluded about the veiled nature of words, "Well-devised riddles are pleasant for the same reason—the solution is an act of learning." For writers, teachers, professionals, psychologists, parents, coaches, or students, riddles are an ingenious way to see with fresh eyes, and have a few startling laughs along the way.

Once we do, with these glimpses of folk wisdom and examples of people who have truly visualized the world, we can resume the unriddling of our most baffling enigma—our own *imagination*—as Lewis Carroll described it in this last stanza of his riddle:

A flashing light—a fleeting shade—
Beginning, end, and middle:
Of all that human art hath made,
Or wit devised! Go, seek *her* aid,
If you would guess her riddle.

II

The Pleasury

1 In marble walls as white as milk,
Lined with skin as soft as silk,
Within a fountain crystal clear,
A golden apple doth appear.
No doors there are to this stronghold,
Yet thieves break in and steal the gold.

—English

2 White as the snow,
Black as the coal,
She walks and she has no feet,
She speaks and has no mouth.

—Mexican

3 I have a basket full of jewels; in the evening
they are strewn and in the morning they are
gathered up.

—Italian

4 Riddle me, riddle me, riddle me,
Perhaps you can tell me what this riddle
    may be:
As deep as a house,
As round as a cup,
And all the king's horses can't draw it up.

—English

5 You are a riddlemaker and you believe yourself
    to be one.
Find me an old woman who is one month old.

—Tuscan (Italy)

6 Crooked as a rainbow,
Teeth like a cat.
I bet a gold fiddle
You caint guess that.

—Ozark (America)

7 What is it—
That we love more than life,
Fear more than death,
The rich want it.
The poor have it,
The miser spends it,
And the spend'rift saves it?

—Antiguan (West Indies)

8 Jack-at-a-word ran over the moor,
Never behind but always before.

—American

9 Tho' blind I am, I lead the blind,
Which way so ever he's inclin'd;
I bear the man who first bears me,
by which name you soon will see.

—English

10 What is it that goes along the foothills on the mountain patting out tortillas with its hands?

—Aztec

11 It has eyes and a nose
But has not breathed since birth;
It cannot go to heaven
And will not stay on earth.
What is it?

—Chinese

12 I am found to be swifter than fire or wind. I travel to unknown worlds which mortal eye has never seen and change them around in the twinkling of an eye.

Icelandic

13 White bird featherless
Flew out from Paradise,
Perched upon yon castle wall.
Up came Lord Landless,
Took it up handless,
And rode away horseless
To the king's white hall.

—Roman

14 Here I am, there I am, and yet they cannot
catch me.

—Bulgarian

15 It is grumbling.
Beyond the mountain smoke is rising;
It chases away the caribou.
What is that?

—Labrador Eskimo

16 A bright red flower he wears on his head;
His beautiful coat needs no thimble nor
    thread;
And though he's fearsome, I'll have you know
Ten thousand doors open when he says no!
What is it?

—*Chinese*

17 Hickamore, Hackamore
On the king's kitchen door;
All the king's horses
And all the king's men
Couldn't drive Hickamore, Hackamore
Off the king's kitchen door!

—*American*

18 A race of young colts. Without running, I can't
    catch them;
without catching, I can't hold them.

—*Portuguese*

19 A young lady was walking through the
        meadow and scattered her golden pearls.
    The Moon saw this, yet didn't tell her.
    The Sun woke up and gathered the pearls.

    —Lithuanian

20 There is a place where a lasso sits.

    —Amuzgo (Oaxaca, Mexico)

21 There is a woman who is always scolding
        everything.
    She is very ugly, and so is her husband.

    —Bolivian-Peruvian

22 The cow gave it birth,
It grew in the wood,
Yet the smith made it.

—Gaelic

23 What has ears yet cannot hear?
—Lancandon (Guatemala)

24 There is also a person, who is small and real
fat, and who has a black face.
He has the habit of eating a lot of bread.
What is it?

—Bolivian

25 The living desire it, and those who have it
    are rarely cheerful and contented with it.

                        —Javanese

26 I met a little boy and he was crying. I axed him
    why.
    He said his mother died six months before he
    was born.

                  —African American

27 What is the wink that inspires fear?

                      —Philippine

28 It conquers the tiger, it conquers the lion, and
        it conquers the enraged bull;
    It conquers men and kings. They all fall, over-
        come, at its feet.

                              —*Spanish*

29 I planted black rice in white earth;
    It could not be harvested by a knife but only
        by the mind.

                              —*English*

30 Ask what is my name, useful to men;
    my name is famous, of service to men,
    sacred in myself.

                              —*Anglo-Saxon*

31 What is that?
A towel sown with silk.
No one ever took it into his hands.
In the field a piece of silk in five colors.
Neither you nor I can grasp it.
On the sky there hangs a kerchief in red colors,
so it is said.

—*Nordic*

32 What is it that which goes up the hill
And down the hill,
And of all yet standeth still?

—*Canadian*

33 Just two hairs grow upon her head,
But she wears a flowered gown
And dances along the flower bed—
The prettiest creature in town!

—*Chinese*

34 I have a tree of great honor,
Which tree beareth both fruit and flower;
Twelve branches this tree hath make,
Fifty-two nests therein he make,
And every nest hath birds seven;
Thank-ed be the King of Heaven;
And every bird hath a different name:
How may all this together frame?

—*Old English*

35 It's between heaven and earth and is not on a tree,
In this riddle I have told you but you can't tell
me.

—*American*

36 It is a beautiful house with twelve rooms and
thirty people can sleep in each room. There are
four doors left open. Have you ever passed
through these doors?

—*Burmese*

37 I stand on four legs, my arms turned toward
       people.
    High and low bow for me,
    but I never bow for anyone.

                              —*Icelandic*

38 Tear one off and scratch my head,
    What once was red is black instead.

                              —*American*

39 What is it that a young man can give a maiden
    That he does not have,
    That he cannot have, that he has never had,
    That he will never have,
    And that he cannot give to a young man?

                              —*Breton*

40 When I went through the garden gap,
Whom should I meet but Dick Red-Cap,
A stick in his hand, a stone in his throat,
Guess me this riddle and I'll give you a groat.

—English

41 What is it that belongs to you,
But others use it more than you do?

—American

42 Two sisters sit at the upstairs windows,
They look around, but cannot see each other.

—Philippine

43 They are two brothers. However much they run,
they do not reach each other.

—Persian

44 Find it, find it, the riddle,
The blazing riddle.
Its shadow is of silver,
The burning riddle.

—Koman (Turkey)

45 She fell but was not broken, though two or
more pieces were there.
Without wings she flew away.
O wise one, think about it.

—Gujarti Indian

46 The stones, the far-throwers.

—African

47 Thirty white horses
Upon a red hill,
Now they tramp,
Now they champ,
Now they stand still.

—English

48 Smaller than a mouse and higher than a castle.

—Welsh Gypsy

49

49 A body met a body
In a bag of beans,
Said a body to a body,
"Can a body tell a body
What a body means?"

—American

50 That which digs about in the deserted village.
—Lamba (Africa)

51 There is that person; if you eat his mouth, he'll
also eat your mouth.

—Amuzgo (Oaxaca, Mexico)

52 Of us five brothers at the same time born,
Two from our birthday our beards have worn,
On other two none ever have appeared,
While the fifth brother wears but half a beard.

—English

53 The king's child looks down from above.

—Malagaian (Madagascar)

54 Who can that blond lady be
With her hair streaming behind her?
She rushes through flower-starred fields
Without guide or companion.

—Spanish

55 I wrote, *wrote, wrote,*
I wrote on five sticks
I kneaded my mercury,
I wrapped my *green* silk.

—*Turkish*

56 What force cannot get through,
I, with a gentle touch, can do;
And many in the street would stand,
Were I not, as a friend, at hand.

—*Ontarian (Canada)*

57 Black crows on a white bank. They are saying,
Caw! Caw!

—*Kashmiri*

58 The little chap who plays the typewriter.

—Philippine

59 From five feet high,
Up to the sky,
It reaches, tho' 'tis round.
Now try your Wits,
If fancy hits,
This Riddle you'll expound.

—Old English

60 Adam an' Eve an' Pinchme
All fell spang in th' creek;
Adam an' Eve was drownded,
Who got out?

—Ozark (America)

61 Riddle, riddle me, Randy Row,
My father gave me some seeds to sow;
The seeds were black, the ground was white,
Riddle me that against Saturday night.

—American

62 What is a cardinal going first and a crow
following behind?

—Aztec

63 What sits on the stove without burning itself?
What sits on the table and is not ashamed?
What goes through a keyhole without pinch-
ing itself?

—American

64 The young men with the white headdresses,
who are in a row.

— Southern Sotho (Africa)

65 Twelve brothers and sisters with only one
father and mother,
One intestine and one stomach, one heart and
two arms;
But including the parents, they all add to one
when you count them.

—Philippine

66 Old Mother Twitchett had but one eye,
And a long tail which she let fly,
And every time she went over a gap,
She left a bit of her tail in a trap.

—English

67 At birth I was green
But I was dressed in a thousand colors,
I have caused many deaths,
And imprisoned many men.

—Dominican

68 Arthur O'Bower has broken his band
And he comes roaring up the land;
The King of Scots with all his power
Cannot stop Arthur of the Bower.

—Scottish

69 All my life I am a priest, after death I am a
cardinal.

—Italian

70 The highest one is alive, the lowest one is
   alive, the one between is dead and weeps and
   makes white meal.

   —*Breton*

71 When I was taken from the fair body,
   They cut off my head,
   And then my shape was altered;
   It's I that make peace between king and king.
   And many a true lover glad:
   All this I do and ten times more,
   And more I could do still,
   But nothing can I do,
   Without my guide's will.

   —*English*

72 Many lights, no one can turn them on.

   —*Chilean*

73 What is that which goes out of the body when death comes in?

—*Tasaday (Philippines)*

74 Flying it appears like a hankerchief;
Landing it appears like a closed fist.

—*Philippine*

75 Two sisters, one black, one white.

—*French West Indian*

76 It barks in the mountains and is silent at home.

—*Argentinian*

77 A dish full of all kinds of flowers,
You can't guess this riddle in two hours.

—*American*

78 What is that: a tree that has neither flower nor
leaf, but of which the fruit is very good?

—*Catalan*

79 As I was going o'er Tipple Tine,
I met a flock of bonny swine;
Some yellow necked,
Some yellow backed,
They were the very bonniest swine
That ever went over Tipple Tine.

—Scottish

80 Three wells and you reach water.

—Hawaiian

81 Wherever I go I give contentment;
But where I am not, there misery is.

—Spanish

82 What lives without a body, speaks without a
   tongue;
   Everyone can hear it, yet no one can see it?

   —*Lithuanian*

83 Brown I am and much admired;
   Many horses have I tired;
   Tire a horse and worry a man;
   Tell me this riddle if you can.

   —*Ontarian (Canada)*

84 The thing which you can hit without leaving a
   scar.

   —*Ronga (Africa)*

85 What is that has three heads, three mouths,
three noses, six eyes, six arms, six ears, and
four legs?

—Korean

86 His cistern full of water and fire lighted atop.
When his flute sounds, there comes forth
a black snake.

—Hindi

87 A beautiful woman
sitting on a cup.

—Philippine

88 Sweetie
fell in love with me
and threw me down on the road.

—Russian

88 What grows without roots?

—Finnish

90 Two bodies have I,
Though both joined in one.
The stiller I stand,
The faster I run.

—American

91 Riddlecum, riddlecum ruckup,
What fell down and stuck up?

—*American*

92 Riddle, riddle,
A very beautiful girl displays her beautiful
    buttocks
In her father's farm.

—*Nigerian*

93 This is a riddle that is entertaining.
What living thing in this world has an intes-
    tine [that is] brilliant?

—*Philippine*

94　The land is white,
　　The sea is black,
　　It'll take a good scholar
　　To riddle me that.

　　　　　　　　　—American

95　As black as ink and isn't ink,
　　As white as milk and isn't milk,
　　As soft as silk and isn't silk,
　　And hops about like a filly-foal.

　　　　　　　　　—English

96　Riddle my riddle rocket,
　　You can't hit it
　　And I can't knock it.

　　　　　　　　　—American

97 At night this flower opens.
    At daytime it gives the honey of happiness.
    It removes the fatigue of men.

                    —*Kannada Indian*

98 Round though not an orange,
    White though not paper,
    Fragrant though not perfume,
    Hot though not ginger.

                    —*Philippine*

99 Two lookabouts,
    Two hookabouts,
    And four bigstanders.

                    —*African American*

100 Nonsense sitting on a chair, with nonsense
     sitting at a table.
Nonsense talks nonsense.

—West Indian

101 Black and white and red all over
Goes from Halifax to Dover.

—Nova Scotian

102 Brass toes
Brass nose.
Upon my soul
It scares the crows.

—American

103 As I was a-walking on Westminster Bridge,
I met with a Westminster scholar;
He pulled off his cap, an' drew off his gloves,
Now what was the name of the scholar?

—English

104 There was a man rode through our town,
Gray Grizzle was his name;
His saddle-bow was gilt and gold,
Three times I've named his name.

—English

105 My mother went over to your mother's house
to borrow
A wim babble, wam bobble, a hind body fore
body, whirl-a-kin nibble.

—American

106 Little Jessie Ruddle
A settin' in a puddle,
Green garters an' yaller toes;
Tell me that riddle or I'll pull yer nose!

—*American*

107 What's the biggest saw you ever saw in a saw
or that anybody said they saw in a saw?

—*African American*

108 Humpty-Dumpty sat on a wall.
Humpty-Dumpty had a great fall.
All the great horses, and all the great men,
Couldn't put Humpty together again.

—*English*

109 As I was going o'er London Bridge,
I heard something crack;
Not a man in all England
Can mend that!

—*English*

110 Two-legs sat on Three-legs by Four-legs.
One leg knocked Two-legs off Three-legs;
Two legs hit Four-legs with Three-legs.

—*American*

111 It was once was low
But now it's high
It once was wet
But now it's dry
It once was black
But now it's red
I put it upstanding
And it fell down dead.

—*Irish*

112 My first is in blue, but not in glue;
My second in old but not in new;
My third in look but not in see
My last in ask but not in plea
My whole has leaves but not a flower
'Twill help you pass an idle hour.

—English

113 The moon nine days old,
The next sign to Cancer;
Pat rat without a tail;
And now, sir, for your answer.

—American

114 Take 500 from the opposite of light, and tell
me where your father's father dwelt in the
time of the Deluge.

—Antiguan (West Indies)

115 Make three-fourths of a cross,
And a circle complete,
And let two semicircles
On a perpendicular meet;
Next add a triangle
That stands on two feet;
Next two semicircles
And a circle complete.

—English

116 There was a donkey tied to a rope,
And the rope was only eight feet long,
But a bunch of carrots was thirty yards away.
How did the donkey get the carrots?

—Arkansan (America)

117 Cornstalks twist your hair.
Mortar and pestle pound you.
Fiery dragons carry you off.
Great cartwheels surround you.

—American

74

118 I've got a beautiful, beautiful hall
All walled in red velvet,
With all white armchairs made of bone,
And in the middle a woman dances.

—Tuscan (Italy)

119 I ride, I ride, no tracks are left;
I chop and chop;
There are no chips left.
He rides and rides;
Turns around:
There is no road left.

—Lithuanian

120 A grassland burns, leaving an old man.

—Mbeere (Africa)

121 I saw some object near to a town,
In a very finely made palace between earth and
heaven.
It has a fine tail which almost reaches to the
ground,
And its tongue hangs in a very large skull.
It spends most of its time in silence,
But sometimes it calls its friends together.

—*Welsh*

122 In the valley is a temple. On the temple sit
two fireflies. Above the fireflies is a hill.
On the hill are tigers and bears.

—*Baiga (India)*

123 Name me and you destroy me.

—*American*

124 I buy a piece of land today.
What is the first thing I put in it?

—*West Indian*

125 Mother lives in the grass, father clings to the
wall, son wanders about in the world.

—*German*

126 A brown stallion that groans, sixty mares
yelling simultaneously with a shrill voice.
They, having developed large udders, foal at
the same time.

—*Mongolian*

127 Two lions are waiting on the hill.

—*Zezuran (Africa)*

128 A child smaller than sheep fills the whole
house.

—*Breton*

129 If they come, it will not come.
But if they do not come, then it will come.

—*Surinamese*

130 What has a tall grandfather and a short father,
a black mother and a white child?

—Mexican

131 It does not know any grammar and it is not
well versed in holy scripture,
but it knows right and wrong. If it is wrong,
its tongue sticks out.

—Burmese

132 Sometimes black, sometimes white.
I have veins, but no blood.

—French

133   Thru a rock, thru a reel
     Thru a hipper, thru a clipper,
     Thru a basin full of pepper,
     Thru an old cow's shin bone,
     A riddle like this was never known.

—Newfoundland

134   What is it that is too much for one,
     Enough for two,
     And nothing at all for three?

—American

135   They cut off its head. They cut off its feet.
     And its middle calls the town together.

—Yoruban (Africa)

136 The crop-eared stallion has the voice of a
one-year or two-year-old colt.

—Mongolian

137 The ox goes with the the wedding-folks.

—Cheremish (Russia)

138 Here's a thing:
Sixteen working,
Sixteen resting,
Two shepherds,
Two listeners,
And one a-staring.

—Maltese

139 Gold under the square field, and comes back white.

—*Faeoric (Denmark)*

140 What is it that fits against your belly and is
    wet when it is in,
dry when it is out, and makes you sweat when
    you work it?

—*Comanche Indian*

141 Two are now many,
Many are now few,
Snows are falling.

—*Polish*

142 A horse with a silver tail neighs on a high hill.

—Lithuanian

143 Robbers came to our house and we were all in.
The house leapt out the windows and we were
all taken.

—Greek

144 When he is small
He is clothed,
When he is grown up,
He is naked.

—Lauan (Melanesia)

145   You face south, it faces north.
      You appear sad, it is also sad.
      You appear glad, it is also glad.

                          —Chinese

146   An old man shuck it and shuck it
      and an old lady pulled up her
      dress and took it.

                          —American

147   She is someone who can entertain;
      It is well known that she dances well;
      I am one of those who look on her;
      It is indeed a great wonder—she dances nude.

                          —Philippine

148 Flesh at both ends,
Iron and wood in the middle.

—Pennsylvania Dutch (America)

149 What is deeper than the deepest sea?

—Swedish

150 I part the fur, I thrust in [something] warm.

—Mongolian

151 Without smooth as glass,
Within a woolly mass,
Bid hid amid a wool,
There lurks a nice mouthful.

—Macedonian (Greece)

152 A black garden with white corn.

—Kgatlan (Africa)

153 Has many shields and spears, but can't defend
wife and children.

—Malagasy

154 Chip, chip, cherry,
All the men in Derry
Can't climb chip, chip, cherry.

—*Irish*

155 Four stunning feet I have and hands a pair,
Unlike myself, not one and one I fare,
I ride and walk at once, for me two bodies bear.

—*Roman*

156 Where does a crow fly when it is six years old?
—*South African*

157 Green but not a lizard, white without being
snow,
and bearded without being a man.

—*Basque*

158 Many people come from the jungle and make
small huts, living together.
Stronger people come and kill them and take
away their food.

—*Ceylonese*

159 What doth with his roote upwards grow,
and downward with his head doth show?

—*Old English*

160 A thing you do not wish to enter but into
which you must go by force.

—Maltese

161 When the golden one splits, it falls standing on
its feet.
My red silk cloth falls spreading out.

—Turkish

162 There was a girl in our town,
Silk an' satin was her gown,
Silk an' satin, gold an' velvet,
Guess her name, three times I've telled it.

—English

163 Old Mother Old,
She lives in the cold,
And every year she brings forth young,
And every one without a tongue.

—Nova Scotian

164 One puts it in white, one takes it out red.

—Greek

165 What is it that runs around the house?

—Ainu (Japan)

166 Long, swift daughter of the forest and borne
along,
With an innumerable throng of companions
equally encompassed,
I speed over many paths, leaving not a trace
behind.

—Roman

167 Somet'in follow you ev'whey you go.
—African American
Sea Islands, South Carolina (America)

168 The wolf and the bear sit across from each
other.

—Cheremish (Russia)

92

169 What is that: the father is not yet born, and the
son is already running on the roof?

—*Catalan*

170 A parrot dancing on a shelf full of cowries
[shells].

—*Punjabi (India)*

171 I am born in the sea, neither bird nor fish.
If my flesh is removed I can be your playmate.

—*Philippine*

172 There is that person whose teeth are all in its stomach.

—*Amizgo (Oaxaca, Mexico)*

173 Two brothers we are; great burdens we bear,
By which we are heavily pressed;
The truth is to say, we are full all the day,
And empty when we go to rest.

—*English*

174 The chief moves slowly
Among his waiting people.

—*Venda (South Africa)*

175 A little thing that dresses in white calico,
When it enters the water,
It does not even get wet.

—*Lamba (Africa)*

176 My house has one beam and two doors.

—*Hawaiian*

177 Thrown to the floor,
The nose was hit.
Aimed at the feet,
The nose was hit.

—*Philippine*

178 Old Mr. Chang, I've heard it said,
You wear a basket on your head;
You've two pair of scissors to cut your meat,
And two pairs of chopsticks with which you
    eat.
What is it?

—Chinese

179 Riddledy, riddledy, riddledy rout,
What does a little boy hold in his hand
When he goes out?

—Ozark (America)

180 A numerous herd of horses has its pasture
ground in the northwest.

—Mongolian

181 He goes with you to the door and then you put it in your pocket.

—*Arabic*

182 It has many eyes, and mornings and evenings it weeps white tears.

—*Lappish (Lapland)*

183 He hits the Buddha with willow branches.

—*Mongolian*

184 He accompanies you constantly, and you pay
him nothing.

—Arabic

185 White as snow but snow it's not,
Green as grass but grass it's not,
Red as blood but blood it's not,
Black as ink but ink it's not.
What is it?

—American

186 The water is in the lake and the snake is in the
water.
Golden color is reflected from the mouth of
the snake.

—Burmese

187 What is it that has two sides and a thousand
ribs?

—*American*

188 A long white barn,
Two roofs on it,
And no door at all, at all.

—*Irish*

189 Down under the hill there was a mill;
In the mill there was a chest,
And in the chest there was a till;
In the till there was a cup,
And in the cup there was a drop.
No man could drink it,
No man could eat it,
No man could do without it.

—*American*

190 Riddle-me-ree,
     Locked up inside you
     And yet they can steal it from you.

                              —*Maltese*

191 Soon as I am made I'm sought with care;
     For one week a year consulted;
     The time elapsed, I'm thrown aside,
     Neglected and insulted.

                              —*English*

192 I see it and don't smoke it, walking on top of
         the coals,
     the dew doesn't wet it, and it doesn't travel
         alone.

                              —*Irish*

193 A bluish horse with perspiring sides.

—Mongolian

194 Abroad wood was being hewn, here the chips
are falling.

—Lettish (Latvia)

195 Within the skin is the hide, within the hide is
the bone, within the bone
is the flesh, and within the flesh is the blood.

—Puerto Rican

196 House full, yard full,
Can't catch a spoonfull.

—American

197 Old Father Boris came to the door,
He came with a dash and a rush and aroar.
He whooped and he hollered,
and he made a great din,
And at last the old fellow
popped right in.

—English

198 A silver pipe is playing, the tsar's gate opens,
the earthworm moves.

—Cheremish (Russia)

199 A soldier stands on a hill armed with a hundred swords.

—Finnish

200 Who are these two lords
who are pursuing each other
and never meet?

—Luba (Africa)

201 The masters of the estate will eat their own laborers.

—Italian

202   Big as a barn,
      Light as a feather,
      And sixty horses can't pull it.

                  —American

203   Red and blue, purple and green,
      No one can reach it,
      Not even a queen.

                  —English

204   As I was going through my grandfather's lot,
      I saw something that made me squat,
      It looked so sweet and tasted so sour,
      You can't guess that in half an hour.

                  —American

205 There is something that goes along—
and turns to look behind.

—Welsh

206 Men will take pleasure in seeing their own
work worn out and destroyed.

—Italian

207 What is that good-looking person in a white-
striped blanket?

—Comanche Indian

208 Broad-arse, thin-waisted, sparkling eyes.

—*Cheremish (Russia)*

209 What are the ten thin slabs of stone that one is always hauling around?

—*Aztec*

210 A marvel, a marvel!
What can it be?
It is born in the mountain
And lives on the water.

—*Spanish*

211 Even if I do not come looking for it, it will
come looking for me.

—Philippine

212 Good morning, good morning to your
ceremony, Mr. King.
I drunk a drunk out of your morning spring
Through the gold the stream did run,
In your garden the stream was done;
If you can onriddle that I'll be hung.

—American

213 Love I sit,
Love I stand,
Love I hold,
Fast in hand.
I see Love,
Love sees not me,
Riddle me that
Or hanged I'll be.

—American

214 As I was going to St. Ives
I met a man with seven wives,
Each wife had seven sacks,
Each sack had seven cats,
Each cat had seven kits.
Kits, cats, sacks, and wives,
How many were going to St. Ives?

—English

215 Riddlum, riddlum, raddy,
All head and no body.

—American

216 What is,
An old woman
With a belly on her face?

—Mexican

217 My boat is turned up at both ends;
All storms it meets it weathers.
On its body you'll find not a single board,
For it's covered all over with feathers.
Daily we fill it with rice;
It's admired by all whom we meet.
You will find not a crack in my boat,
But you'll find underneath it two feet.
What is it?

—Chinese

218 As I went over Heeple Steeple
I met up with a heap o' people,
Some was nicky, some was nacky,
Some was the color of brown tabacky.

—American

219 There is a place with a cut-down tree in the big
river.

—Amizgo (Oaxaca, Mexico)

220 Old Grandfather Diddle Daddle
Jumped in the mudpuddle,
Green cap and yellow shoes.
Guess all your loftiness
And you can't guess these news.

—American

221 Goes 'round the house and 'round the house
And drops a white glove at each window.

—English

222 There was a man on earth,
He had no dwelling-place dere,
Neither in heaven nor in hell.
Tell me where that man did dwell.

—American

223 Round as a biscuit,
Busy as a bee,
Prettiest little thing
I ever did see.

—*American*

224 In a turquoise-blue field
Marvelous beauties are flowering,
But so capricious are they
That only at night do they glow.

—*Spanish*

225 My single quiver,
My innumerable arrows.

—*Turkish*

226 Behind the king's kitchen there is a great vat,
   And a great many workmen working at that.
   Yellow are their toes, yellow are their clothes.
   Tell me this riddle and you can pull my nose.

                              —*American*

227 A serpentine of gold;
   Nobody wants it,
   Although it may be worth a fortune.

                              —*Spanish*

228 In the deserted plain a tortise died,
   A whole village mourned it.

                              —*Marathi (Indian)*

229 Two big biscuits, one cup of coffee,
Gwine to Augusta black and dirty.

—African American

230 We tie and carry bundles without knowing the
contents.

—Camaroonese

231 A multicolored door,
The handle of a chain.
It has five branches,
It has one leaf.

—Azerbaijani

232 Something white as cotton, green as grass, and
blue as ink, and sweet as sugar.

—American

233 The box opened. Hazelnuts scattered.

—Ottoman (Turkey)

234 What has roots as nobody sees,
Is taller than trees,
Up, up it goes,
And never goes?

—English

235 What is a little mirror in the middle of fir
trees?

—*Aztec*

236 In Central Park I saw Uncle Jack,
Walking along with the world on his back.

—*American*

237 One seizes it, one opens it, but one doesn't
carry it away.

—*Indonesian*

238 My veiled face is my face itself; unveiled it is
annulled.
I am hidden and concealed, yet if you discover
me,
I will disappear before your eyes forever.

—Italian

239 Two lovers are barred from every joy and bliss,
Who through the live-long night embracing
lie:
They guard the folk from calamities,
But with the rising sun apart they fly.

—Arabic

240 A young lady is standing, wearing a pretty hat;
whoever walks past her, bows their head low.

—Lithuanian

241 Now it's here and now it's not.

—Serbian

242 My first is in dress, but not in robe
My second in map, but not in globe;
My third in mirth, but not in glee
My fourth in plant, but not in tree.
My fifth in smart, but not in brain
My last in mask, but not in feign
The whole of me sometimes you'll find
On tables that are most refined.

—Near Eastern

243 I'm in everybody's way,
But no one I stop;
My four horns every day
In every way play,
And my head is nailed on at the top.

—English

244 A shoemaker makes shoes without leather,
With all the four elements together,
Fire, Water, Earth, Air,
And every customer takes two pair.

—*English*

245 There is a person standing on one leg who has
no face, although he has a head.
He lives for only one day.

—*Ceylonese*

246 What weeps without eye or eyelid, her tears
rejoicing sons and fathers—
And when she laughs and no tears fall, her
laughter saddens all hearts.

—*Hebrew*

247 Went clear to the woods to get it,
Didn't like it after I got it,
The longer I had it the less I liked it,
Still got it because I can't help it.

—Arkansan (America)

248 What are they that go pushing along wrinkled
faces?

—Aztec

249 Long shins, crooked thighs, [and]
a wee small skull without an eye.

—Irish

250 Soldiers without souls fight without pay.

—Mongolian

251 Large, small, sweet, bitter.

—Languedoc (France)

252 On the hill there is a mill,
Round the mill there is a walk,
Under the walk there is a key.

—American

253   What is deeper than the sea?

—Irish

254   Big at each end and little in the middle,
Digs up the dirt and sings like a fiddle.

—American

255   The gnome that boils over.

—Lamba (Africa)

256 What goes to the bayou laughing and returns
crying?

—Cajun American

257 Two arrows with black wings reach wherever
they wish.

—Albanian

258 Green in the mountains,
black in the plaza,
red in the house.

—Guatemalan

259   What we caught we threw away;
       what we could not catch we kept.

—Ancient Greek

260   This thing all things devours:
       Birds, beasts, trees, flowers;
       Gnaws iron, bites steel;
       Grinds hard stones to meal;
       Slays king, ruins town,
       And beats high mountain down.

—English

261   About six inches long, an' a mighty pretty size;
       Not a lady in the country but what will take it
         between her thighs.

—American

262 Over there smoke goes up.
Over there smoke goes up.

—*Thonga (Africa)*

263 I washed my hands in water
That never rained nor un;
I dried them with a towel
That was never wove nor spun.

—*American*

264 What are the birds which graze on a place not
near?

—*South American*

265 Two brothers run away, and two others try to
catch them, but never can.

—Polish

266 Upon the hill there is a yellow house;
Inside the yellow house there is a cream house;
Inside the cream house there is a pink house;
And inside the pink house there's a lot of little
white babies.

—American

267 Boys, sweep the yard so Mr. Finger-Pointer
can dance.

—Shona (Africa)

268 She sits upon a porch rocking in a chair, her
apron strings won't tie.
What is she doing?

—American

269 What is the strongest of all things?

—Ancient Greek

270 The beginning of the story [riddle] is in
Turkish;
The meaning is expounded correctly;
It is dear to the author;
It cannot be expounded in the present world.

—Mongolian

271 The beginning of eternity,
The end of time and space,
The beginning of every end
And the end of every place.

—*English*

272 At the top of a long pole
A bird called Urguul sits.
To throw it down, one has to be a man.
One has to be quick of heart.

—*Turkish*

273 It came, though I fetched it; when come it was
  gone,
It stayed but a moment, it could not stay long;
I ask not who saw it, it could not be seen,
And yet might be felt by a king or queen.

—*English*

274 A delusion letter under a pillow.

—Mongolian

275 Soulless one catches soulful.

—Cheremish (Russia)

276 There she goes over the road.
A young mare that is whinnying.
A fiery spot on her forehead.
With her hindquarters ablaze.

—Irish

277 When I went up Sandy-Hill,
I met a sandy-boy;
I cut his throat, I sucked his blood,
And left his skin a-hanging-o.

—English

278 Guess what it is that very often goes and
moves and yet does not
depart from its place.

—French

279 Don't meddle, don't touch,
Little girl, little boy,
Or the world will lose
Some of its joy.

—American

280 When I was alive I fed the living. Now I am
dead; I carry the living, and over the living do
I go.

—French

281 I went into my grandmother's garden,
And there I found a farthing.
I went into my next door neighbor's
There I bought a pipkin and a popkin,
A slipkin and a slopkin,
A nailboard, a sailboard,
And all for a farthing.
Throw it up green, comes down red.

—English

282 There is a place that is cut up by gullies.

—Omaha Indian

283 What is the longest and yet the shortest thing
     in the world,
The swiftest and yet the slowest, the most
     divisible and the most extended,
The least valued and the most regretted,
     without which nothing can be done,
Which devours everything, however small, and
     yet opens the life and spirit
To every object, however great?

                     —English

284 We are little airy creatures,
All of different voice and features;
One of us in glass is set,
One of us you'll find in jet,
T'other you may see in tin,
And the fourth a box within.
If the fifth you should pursue,
It can never fly from you.

                     —Irish

285 The son begins to sail, while the father is not yet born.

—Swedish

286 What is it that thing which you cannot hold for five minutes, yet it is light as a feather?

—American

287 Under the ground, a moon travels.

—Kazakh Tatar

288 Clink! The sieve! Clank! The iron sheet;
At night he is full, by day his stomach empty.

—Ottoman (Turkey)

289 It increases and decreases,
And no one sees it.
It is not a fire,
And yet it can be quenched.

—American

290 There is a little mystic clock,
    No human eye hath seen;
That beateth on—and beateth on,
    From morning until e'en. . . .

—German

291 Companion of a god, the depths I'm always
    near,
I to the Muses sing and black appear,
By min'string fingers pressed, give the tongue's
    message clear.

—Roman

292 Crimson of earth, a splendid color dyed,
Take care! Behind a prickly hedge I hide,
O happy, could I longer here abide!

—Roman

293 What is it that is wingless and legless,
Yet flies and cannot be imprisoned?

—American

294 Not hurled, not twisted, but it reaches, it
reaches.

—Malagasian

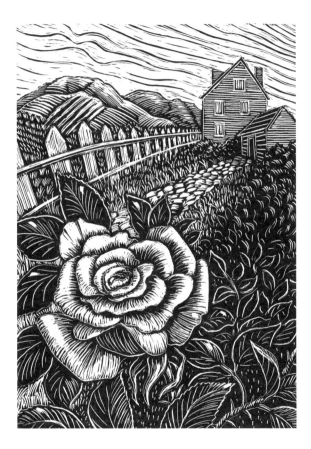

295 Wealth is never exhausted.

—Mbeere (African)

296 From within, silk scattered.

—Kazakh Tatar

297 What's the softest [thing] on earth?

—Cheremish (Russia)

298 It runs and runs and yet does not run away,
     It longs for sunlight but never sees it.

                              —*Gypsy*

299 There is one that walks but leaves no trail.

                              —*Yakut*

300 I am a noble being, known to earls,
     And I rest often with the high and the low,
     Famed among the folk. I fare widely.
     With me at times remote from friends,
     Booty remains, when I glory in the burgs
     And a bright course. Now learned men
     Greatly love my presence.

                              —*Anglo-Saxon*

The Guessery

1. An egg
2. A letter
3. The stars and the sky
4. A well
5. The moon
6. A briar bush
7. Nothing
8. Will-o-the-wisp
9. A walking stick
10. A butterfly
11. A dragon kite
12. Thought or dream

13. The snow and sun [A tenth-century Latin riddle]

14. Mind or thought

15. A boiling kettle. *Children take care!*
    [Traditional warning]

16. A rooster

17. Sunlight. *A hackamore is a saddle.*

18. The wind

19. Dew

20. A rattlesnake

21. A toad

22. Bellows

23. Fire

24. An oven

25. Old age

26. She dyed the boy's clothes.

27. A bolt of lightning.

28. Sleep

29. A letter

30. A book
31. A rainbow
32. A road
33. A butterfly
34. The year [Fifteenth century]
35. A knot on a tree
36. A year
37. A chair
38. A match. [Rhymed by Edward Enigma, aka "The Riddler," to Batman.]
39. The name of a wife
40. A cherry
41. Your name
42. Your own two eyes
43. The wheels of a bicycle
44. That is the butterfly. [Traditional form of response.]
45. The night

46. The eyes

47. Teeth and gums

48. A plum high in a tree

49. Two bugs in a bag of beans [Alliterative American folklore!]

50. The heart—which always turns to think of the past

51. Chili peppers

52. A rosebud

53. A banana bunch

54. A streaking comet

55. That is [applying] henna.

56. Night

57. Paper and ink

58. The tongue

59. The reach of the eyes or eyesight

60. Traditionally, the "chump" says, "Pinchme," and the jokers certainly do.

61. A boy writing in a book

146

62. Something burning

63. The sun

64. Telephone poles

65. Watch or clock

66. Needle and thread

67. A deck of playing cards

68. Wind

69. A crayfish [which is black when living, red when boiled]

70. A sawyer and a log

71. A goose quill pen

72. The stars

73. The part of you that sees the dream: the soul [Gathered by journalist John Nance]

74. A bat

75. Night and day

76. An ax

77. Honey

78. The salt of the sea

79. Bumble bees

80. A coconut

81. Bread

82. An echo

83. A saddle

84. Water

85. A man in a palanquin [An Oriental device for carrying people]

86. A hookah [Many-armed smoking pipe]

87. A cashew [which grows on top of a large, round fruit]

88. Sleep

89. A human being

90. An hourglass

91. A fork

92. A snail [Her shell is her papa's farm; her flesh within is buttock-shaped.]

93. A firefly

94. Paper and ink

95. A magpie

96. Smoke

97. A bed

98. Garlic

99. A cow

100. A man and a rum bottle

101. A newspaper

102. A steam engine

103. "Andrew" was name.

104. "Was" was his name.

105. A spinning wheel

106. A duck in a puddle

107. An "Arkansas"

108. An egg

109. Ice

110. An example of a widespread "leg riddle." An old man sat down on a three-legged stool to milk his cow. When the cow kicked him, he hit her with the stool.

111. Turf or sod

112. A book

113. "Cleopatra," who is hidden in a rebus and charade: C + Leo + pat rat without tail [MG]

114. The Ark. Dark is opposite of light; 500 in Roman letters is D; this leaves Ark.

115. T + o + b + a + c + c + o = tobacco

116. When somebody says "I give up," the riddler sometimes answers, "That's what the other jackass done." Or the riddlee may say, "Why, the donkey just walked over and ate the carrots. The other end of the rope wasn't tied to anything."

117. A train ride

118. A mouth

119. A boat

120. A stone in a field

121. A church bell

122. The human body

123. Silence

124. Your eyes

125. Grape vines

126. A thunderstorm

127. The ears

128. A snail

129. Small birds and rice

130. A piñon nut (bush, stem, shell, and nut)

131. A balance

132. Marble

133. A spider

134. A secret

135. A drum

136. A balalaika

137. Bagpipes

138. The face

139. Wheat and flour

140. A washboard

141. Old age

142. A church bell

143. Fish in a net

144. Bamboo

145. A mirror [From Bao-yu's eighteenth-century book *The Dream of the Red Chamber*]

146. An apple. The man peeled and the apple unpeeled.

147. A violin

148. A farmer and a plough

149. A skirt, which is without bottom

150. The riddler is sticking his hand in his glove.

151. A chestnut

152. The sky and the stars

153. A lemon tree

154. Smoke from a chimney

155. A centaur [Composed by the fifth-century Roman writer Symphosius]

156. To its seventh year!

157. A leek

158. Bees

159. An icicle

160. A coffin

161. "That is the mare has foaled."

162. Anne

163. An apple tree

164. Bread

165. The logs in the wall of a cabin

166. A ship

167. Your shadow

168. The window and the oven

169. Fire and smoke
170. Tongue and teeth [Cowries are seashells.]
171. A seashell
172. A melon
173. A pair of shoes
174. The moon among the stars
175. Steam
176. The nose
177. A fart
178. A rooster
179. The doorhandle
180. The rising stars
181. A shadow
182. A sieve
183. Winking eyelashes
184. A road
185. A blackberry

186. An oil lamp

187. A railroad

188. An egg

189. The heart's blood

190. The heart

191. An almanac

192. A shadow

193. A whetstone

194. Snow

195. A coconut

196. Smoke

197. The wind

198. The cock crows, the gate opens, the people move.

199. An evergreen tree

200. The sun and the moon

201. Oxen [Attributed to Leonardo da Vinci]

202. The shadow of the barn

203. A rainbow

204. The cranberry

205. A horseshoe

206. A shoesmith [Another of Leonardo's riddles]

207. A skunk

208. A lamp

209. The fingernails

210. A canoe

211. Fate

212. In this North Carolina version of an old "neck-riddle" [a term coined by Archer Taylor for those riddles that literally save someone's neck], a king promises a slave freedom if he can make a riddle that the King cannot "onriddle," or solve. The slave tells him here that he took the Queen out into the garden and drank from her breasts through her gold wedding ring. The king freed him.

213. A well-bred lady condemned to death earned her freedom with this "neck-riddle." She had a dog named "Love"; she killed it and made socks of its skin. She stood on them, and with her gloves she held the seat of her chair. She looked at the gloves and "Love," but now "Love" saw her no more.

214. One: I myself

215. A tadpole

216. A guitar

217. A wild duck

218. An anthill

219. An alligator

220. A frog

221. Snow

222. Jonah in the whale

223. A watch

224. The stars

225. The sky and the stars

226. Bees making honey

227. Lightning

228. An eclipse of the sun

229. A locomotive

230. Pregnancy

231. A hand

232. A huckleberry

233. Camel droppings

234. A mountain [Propounded in *The Hobbit,* by J. R. R. Tolkien]

235. Our eyes

236. A turtle

237. A nut

238. A riddle [Posed by Galileo]

239. The leaves of a door. [From "The Tale of Abu al-Hsun and his Slave Girl Tawaddun" in *The Arabian Nights Entertainment*]

240. A strawberry

241. A spark

242. Damask

243. A turnstile

244. A blacksmith

245. A mushroom

246. A cloud

247. A thorn

248. The knees

249. A pair of tongs

250. Chess pieces

251. An olive

252. Milwaukee

253. A tailor's thimble or a woman's mind

254. A "dirt-dauber," or mosquito

255. A pot of beer

256. A bucket

257. The eyes

258. Charcoal

259. The louse. According to legend, Homer asked two young boys just returning from a fishing trip what they caught, and they answered riddle-style. The poet died from shame because he could not guess the answer.

260. Time [Traditional, but also used by J. R. R. Tolkien in *The Hobbit*]

261. The lefthand horn on a lady's sidesaddle

262. Over there they mourn a chief, over there they mourn a poor man.

263. The dew and the sun

264. The eyes

265. The four wheels of a car or wagon

266. A cantaloupe

267. It is a diviner.

268. A pregnant woman is mourning last year's laughter.

269. Love. Iron is strong, but a blacksmith is stronger. Love can overcome a blacksmith.

270. The Sacred Book

271. The letter *e*

272. The soul

273. A sigh

274. A dream

275. A weir. An inanimate dam catches the animate fish.

276. Thunder

277. An orange

278. The great wheel of a water mill

279. A bird's nest

280. An oak tree, out of which one builds a ship

281. Watermelon

282. An old woman's face

283. Time

284. The Vowels. [From Jonathan Swift's poem "A Riddle"]

285. Smoke and fire

286. Your breath

287. A plowshare

288. A fasting person

289. Thirst

290. The soul

291. The reed [Symphosius]

292. The rose [Symphosius]

293. The voice

294. Your mind or thought

295. Wealth never exhausted is the thought in the heart of a person.

296. The sun through the clouds

297. The hands, for you lean your head on your hands to put yourself to sleep
298. The heart
299. Fog
300. The moon

IV

The Sourcery

The origin of certain riddles is itself a riddle that does not have its Oedipus, although perhaps it one day will; this is so because the way in which riddles traveled through different peoples and races, through hidden and unknown passages, can still be investigated and, if investigated, they can be retraced and collected.

—*Giuseppe Pitre, Italiana scholar,* Indovinelli, dubbi
schioglilingua del popolo siciliano

Because riddles have metamorphosed many times over, it can difficult to cite definitively the origins of many riddles. It is possible, however, to cite at least the sources for many of the riddles in this collection, even those I have heard firsthand from many people around the world. Every possible effort has been made to track down the original sources, so that interested readers may continue their exploration of this enigmatic topic.

If there have been any omissions, corrections will be made in future editions.

Arberry, A. J. *A Maltese Anthology.* Oxford: Clarendon Press, 1960.

Ashu, Comfort Eneke. *Cameroon Riddles and Folklore for School.* Limbe: Nooremar Press, 1984.

Bacon, A. M., and E. C. Parsons. "Folklore from Elizabeth City County." *Journal of American Folklore* 35 (1922).

Balaseviciute, Nomeda. *Menu Menu Misle.* Vilnius: Pegasas, 1991.

Baring-Gould, William S., and Ceil Baring-Gould. *The Annotated Mother Goose.* New York: World Publishing Company, 1962.

Bhagwat, Durga. *The Riddle in Indian Life Lore and Literature.* Bombay: Popular Prakashaw, 1965.

Boas, Franz. "Two Eskimo Riddles from Labrador." *Journal of American Folklore* 39 (1926).

Boggs, R. S. "North Carolina White Folktales and Riddles." *Journal of American Folklore* 47 (1934).

The Book of Meery Riddles. London, 1629. Reprinted in J. O. Halliwell-Phillips, *Literature of the Sixteenth and Seventeenth Century.* London, 1851.

Brunvand, Jan Harold. *The Study of American Folklore: An Introduction.* New York: W. W. Norton & Company, Inc., 1968.

Carter, Isabel G. "Mountain White Riddles." *Journal of American Folklore* 47 (1934).

Cerf, Bennett. *Bennett Cerf's Book of Riddles.* New York: Beginner Books, 1960.

Clarke, Kenneth, and Mary Clarke. *A Folklore Reader.* A. S. Barnes and Co., 1965.

Cocchiara, Giuseppe. *The History of Folklore in Europe.* Translated by John N. McDaniel. Philadelphia: Institute for the Study of Human Issues, 1981.

Coffin, Tristram Potter, and Hennig Cohen. *Folklore from the Working Folk in America.* New York: Anchor Press, 1973.

Crossley-Holland, Kevin, trans. *Storm and Other English Riddles.* New York: Farrar, Straus & Giroux, 1970.

Cuthbertson, W. F., ed. *Rhyme a Riddle.* London: n.p, 1946.

Dorson, Richard M. *American Folklore.* Chicago: University of Chicago Press, 1959.

———. *Negro Tales from Pine Bluff, Arkansas, and Calvin, Michigan.* Bloomington: Indiana University Press, 1958.

Dundes, Alan. *The Study of Folklore.* Englewood Cliffs, NJ: Prentice-Hall, Inc., 1965.

Dundes, Alan, and Maung Than Sein. "Riddles from Central Burma," *Journal of American Folklore* 77 (1964).

Edwards, G. D. "Items of Armenian Folklore Collected in Boston." *Journal of American Folklore* 12 (1899).

Emmeneau, M. B., and Archer Taylor, "Annamese, Arabic, and Panjabi Riddles." *Journal of American Folklore* 58 (1945).

Emrich, Duncan. *The Hodpodge Book.* New York: Four Winds Press, 1972.

———. *The Nonsense Book of Riddles, Rhymes, Tongue Twisters, Puzzles and Jokes from American Folklore.* New York: Four Winds Press, 1970.

Espy, Willard. *The Game of Words.* New York: Horizon Press, 1952.

Espinosa, A. M. "New Mexican Spanish Folklore, IX: Riddles." *Journal of American Folklore* 28 (1915).

Eugenio, Damiana L., ed. *The Riddles: Philippine Folk Literature,* vol V. Quezon City: University of Philippines Press, 1994.

Evans, David. "Riddling and the Structure of Context." *Journal of American Folklore* 89 (1976).

The Exeter Book of Riddles. Translated by Kevin Crossley-Holland. London: Penguin Classics, 1978.

Falassi, Alessandro. *Folklore by the Fireside: Text and Context of the Tuscan Veglia.* Austin: University of Texas Press, 1980.

Farr, T. J. "Riddles and Superstitions of Middle Tennessee." *Journal of American Folklore* 48 (1935).

Fauset, A. H. "Negro Folk-Tales from the South." *Journal of American Folklore* 40 (1927).

———. "Folklore from Nova Scotia." *Memoirs of the American Folklore Society,* 24. New York, 1931.

Finley, H. H. "Folklore from Eleuthera, Bahamas." *Journal of American Folklore* 38 (1925).

Frazer, James G. *The Golden Bough: A Study in Magic and Religion,* abridged ed. New York: Macmillan Co., 1940.

Georges, Robert A., and Alan Dundes. "Toward A Structural Definition of the Riddle." *Journal of American Folklore* 76 (1963).

Goldstein, Kenneth S. "Riddling Traditions in Northeastern Scotland." *Journal of American Folklore* 76 (1963).

Greenway, John. *Folklore of the Great West.* Palo Alto: American West Publishing Co., 1969.

Halliwell-Phillips, James O. *The Nursery Rhymes of England.* London: Warne & Company, 1842.

Haring, Lee. "Malagasy Riddling," *Journal of American Folklore* 98 (1985).

Hart, Donn V. *Riddles in Filipino Folklore: An Anthropological Analysis.* Syracuse: Syracuse University Press, 1964.

Hasan-Rokem, Galit, and David Shulman, eds. *Untying the Knot: On Riddles and Other Enigmatic Modes.* Oxford: Oxford University Press, 1996.

Hassell, James Woodrow, Jr. *Amorous Games: A Critical Edition of Les Adevineaux Amoureux.* Austin: University of Texas Press, published for the American Philosophical Society, 1954.

Hubp, Loretta Burke, trans. *¿Que Sera? What Can It Be?: Traditional Spanish Riddles.* New York: John Day, 1970.

Hull, Vernam E., and Archer Taylor. *A Collection of Irish Riddles.* Berkeley: University of California Folklore Studies 6, University of California Press, 1955.

———. "A Collection of Welsh Riddles." *University of California Publications in Modern Philology* 26 (1942).

Johnson, John H. "Folklore from Antigua, British West Indies." *Journal of American Folklore* 34 (1921).

Knab, T. J., ed. *A Scattering of Jade: Stories, Poems, and Prayers of the Aztecs.* Translated by Thelma D. Sullivan. New York: Simon & Schuster, 1994.

Köngäs-Maranda, Elli. "Riddles and Riddling." *Journal of American Folklore* 89 (1976).

Leach , Maria, and Jerome Fried, eds. *Funk & Wagnalls Standard Dictionary of Folkore, Mythology, and Legend.* San Francisco: HarperSanFrancisco, 1982.

Leland, Charles Godfrey. *The Hundred Riddles of the Fairy Bellaria.* London: T. Fisher Unwin, 1902.

Lucas, Dolores Dyer. *Emily Dickinson and the Riddle.* DeKalb: Northern Illinois University Press, 1969.

McAllester, David P. "Riddles and Other Verbal Play Among the Comanches." *Journal of American Folklore* 78 (1964).

McCollum, Katherine Ann, and Kenneth W. Porter, eds. "Winter Evenings in Iowa, 1873–1880." *Journal of American Folklore* 56 (1943).

Morrison, Lillian. *Black Within and Red Without: A Book of Riddles.* New York: Thomas Y. Crowell, 1952.

Ohl, Raymond T., ed. *The Enigmas of Symphosius.* Philadelphia: n.p., 1928.

Opie, Iona, and Peter Opie. *The Oxford Nursery Rhymes.* London: Oxford University Press, 1951.

Parsons, Elsie Clews. "Bermuda Folklore." *Journal of American Folklore* 38 (1925).

———. "Folklore from Aiken, South Carolina." *Journal of American Folklore* 34 (1921).

———. "Folklore from Antigua, British West Indies." *Journal of American Folklore* 34: 2 (1921).

———. "Folklore of the Antilles, III." *Memoirs of the American Folklore Society,* XXVI, Part 3. New York, 1943.

———. "Riddles from Andros Island, Bahamas." *Journal of American Folklore* 32 (1919).

Perkins, A. E. "Riddles from Negro School-Children in New Orleans." *Journal of American Folklore* 35 (1922).

Pongweni, Alec J. C., and Emmanuel Chiwome. *Traditional and Modern Shona Riddles.* Harare: Juta Zimbabwe, Ltd., 1995.

Potter, Beatrix. *The Tale of Squirrel Nutkin.* London: Penguin Group, 1991.

Potter, Charles Francis. "Riddles." Excerpted from *Funk & Wagnalls Standard Dictionary of Folklore, Mythology, and Legend.* Edited by Maria Leach. San Francisco: HarperSanFrancisco, 1984.

Randolph, Vance, *The Talking Turtle and Other Folk Tales.* New York: Columbia University Press, 1957.

Randolph, Vance, and Isabel Spradley. "Ozark Mountain Riddles." *Journal of American Folklore* 47 (1934).

Redfield, W. A. "A Collection of Middle Tennessee Riddles." *Southern Folklore Quarterly* (1937).

"Riddles and Riddling." *Journal of American Folklore* No. 352 (1976).

Riddles, Charades, and Conundrums: The Greater Part of Which Have Never Been Published, with a Preface on the Antiquity of Riddles. 2d ed. London, 1824.

"Riddles from Ontario, Canada." *Journal of American Folklore* 31 (1918).

Robe, Stanley L. *Index of Mexican Folklore,* 26. Berkeley: University of California Press, 1973.

Rosenblum, Joseph. *The Little Giant Book of Riddles.* New York: Sterling Publishing, Inc., 1996.

Routledge, Edmund, coll. *Riddles and Jokes.* London: George Routledge & Sons, 1924.

Sadovnikou, D. coll. Translated and with an Introduction by Ann C. Bigelow. *Riddles of the Russian People: A Collection of Riddles, Parables, and Puzzles.* Ann Arbor: Ardis Publishers, 1986.

Salny, Abbie F. *The Mensa Book of Words, Word Games, Puzzles & Oddities.* New York: Harper & Row Publishers, 1988.

Schwartz, Alvin. *Unriddling: All Sorts of Riddles to Puzzle Your Guessery.* New York: Harper & Row, 1983.

Scott, Charles T. "New Evidence of American Indian Riddling." *Journal of American Folklore* 54 (1963).

———. *Persian and Arabic Riddles.* Bloomington: Indiana University Press, 1965.

Sebeok, Thomas, ed. *Studies in Cheremis Folklore,* vol I. Bloomington: Indiana University Press, 1952.

Shipley, Joseph T. *Wordplay.* New York: Hawthorn Books, Inc., 1972.

Suzuki, Daisetz Teitaro. *The Zen Koan as a Means of Attaining Enlightenment.* Rutland, VT: Charles E. Tuttle, 1994.

Swann, Brian. "Who Is the East?" *Parabola* (Fall 1988).

Symphosius. *Hundred Riddles.* Translated by Elizabeth Hickman du Bois. Woodstock, VT: The Elm Tree Press, 1912.

Taylor, Archer. *English Riddles from Oral Tradition.* Berkeley and Los Angeles: University of California Press, 1951.

———. *The Literary Riddle Before 1600.* Berkeley and Los Angeles: University of California Press, 1948.

———. *Mongolian Folktales.* The American Philosophical Society. Vol. 44, 1954.

———. "The Riddle." *Studies in Cheremis Folklore,* vol. I. Edited by Thomas Sebeok. Bloomington: Indiana University Press, 1952.

———. "Riddles and Metaphors Among Indian People." *Journal of American Folklore* 49 (1936).

———. "Riddles and Poetry." *SFQ* 11 (1947).

Thompson, Stith. *The Folktale.* New York: Holt, Rinehart, and Winston, Inc., 1946.

Thurston, Helen S. "Riddles from Massachusetts." *Journal of American Folklore* 18 (1905).

Tietze, Andreas. *The Komar Riddles and Turkic Folklore.* Berkeley: University of California Press, 1966.

Vilches, Maria Luz P., ed. *An Annotated Collection of Visayan Riddles.* Tacloban City: Divine Word University Press, 1981.

Waugh, F. W. "Canadian Folklore from Ontario." *Journal of American Folklore* 31 (1918).

Withers, Carl, comp. *A Rocket in My Pocket: The Rhymes and Chants of Young Americans.* New York: Henry Holt & Company, Inc., 1948.

Wyndham, Robert, ed. *Chinese Mother Goose Rhymes.* New York and
    Cleveland: The World Publishing Company, 1968.

Young, Ed., ed. *High on a Hill: A Book of Chinese Riddles.* New York
    and Cleveland: Collins Publishing, 1980.

Zug III, Charles G. "The Nonrational Riddle: The Zen *Koan.*"
    Journal of American Folklore 85 (1963).

V

The Unforgettery

If we should build a "forgettery" into the mansion of our lives, as the poet Carl Sandburg said, perhaps we need to also create an "unforgettery," the place where we are sure not to forget to express our gratitude. These pages constitute such a place so that I might declare my thanks to all those who helped me find solutions to the baffling riddles surrounding the creation of this humble little book.

First, my gratitude goes out to my friends at Conari Press who agreed there was a need for such a work and provided an answer to the conundrum of how to publish it; thanks especially to my publisher Will Glennon and my editor Mary Jane Ryan. Much appreciation, also, to valiant word-warrior Brenda Knight, who helped solve the ancient question: "When one does not know what it is, then it is something; but when one knows what is, then it is nothing." (Answer: A riddle—in literature as well as in life.) Many thanks also to Claudia Smelser for her delightfully elegant book design, to Sharon Donovan and Nancy Margolis for their guidance in finding a market for word puzzles and enigmatic entertainment, and to artist Kathleen Edwards for her captivating illustrations.

My deep gratitude extends to the San Francisco Public Library for the use of the SCOWAH Collection (Schmulowitz Collection of Wit and Humor), the University of California at Berkeley Folklore Department for access to their vast collection on world riddles, and the New York Public Library. Thanks also to the *Journal of American Folklore*, the California Folklore Society, the Western Folklore Society, and the American Folklore Society, for all their efforts in preserving the perennial wisdom of the human race, humorous and otherwise. In my "Unforgettery" I also want to make room for the eminent folklorists Archer Taylor, Peter and I. Opie, Roger D. Abrahams, and Alan Dundes, whose work has inspired me for many years.

Thanks also to all those friends from around the world who contributed their favorite riddles, especially James Van Harper, who led me to many riddles from the American South; Gary Rhine, Reuben Snake (Winnebago), and

Baldwin "Buster" Parker (Comanche), who informed me about the rich vein of riddles among Native Americans; Jaz Lynch, Sean Browne, Colette McGeary, and Myles O'Reilly for their helping me discover the treasure of Irish riddles; Rebecca Armstrong for her lead with the Leonardo da Vinci riddles and rebuses; John Nance for his revelations about riddles in the Philippines; Alexander Eliot for his elucidation of the riddlic nature of the Delphi Oracle; Valerie Andrews for her reminder about the mythic nature of Dame Ragnall's question to Sir Gawain; and *ačiū*, resounding thanks, to Audi Ambrozaitis for her lilting Lithuanian translations.

I am also grateful to my mother, Rosemary M. LaChance Cousineau, for her remembrances of her father's nighttime riddling games during her childhood, especially of traditional English riddles from their turn-of-the-century books with numinous names such as *The Cabinet of Entertainment, Sphinx-Lore,* and *Witty Sayings by Witty People.*

Hearty thanks—*obrigado*—to Beverly McDevitt for the generous gift of her house in Penedo, Portugal, where a very early draft of this work was written; *merci beaucoup* to my friend Jean-Francois Pasquilini for his hospitality in Paris, France, while I researched the provenance of European riddles; and *mille grazie* to all my friends at Caffe Puccini in North Beach, San Francisco, who provided a solution to the riddle of how to stay up all night while completing this manuscript with their strong espresso.

Finally, much love to my companion in this tricksterish world, Jo Beaton, and the source of the gnomic wit in our life, our son, Jack. Without your love and patience, this treasury would have no gold. For you both, a last riddle, from Russia, "You are in me, and I am in you." Answer: *Soul.*

ABOUT THE AUTHOR

Born at an army hospital in Columbia, South Carolina, in 1952, Phil Cousineau grew up just outside of Detroit. While moonlighting in an automotive parts factory, he studied journalism at the University of Detroit. His peripatetic career has included stints as a sportswriter and photographer, playing basketball in Europe, harvesting date trees on an Israeli kibbutz, and painting forty-four Victorian houses in San Francisco.

Cousineau is an author, anthologist, adventure travel leader, teacher, photographer, and documentary filmmaker. His lifelong fascination with the art, literature, and history of culture has taken him on journeys around the world. He lectures frequently on a wide range of topics, from mythology, movies, environmental design, and community work to creativity, mentorship, travel, and soul.

Soul Moments and *The Art of Pilgrimage* are his most recent books. Cousineau is also the author of *Soul: An Archaeology: Readings from Socrates to Ray Charles; Prayers at 3 A.M.; The Soul of the World; Deadlines: A Rhapsody on a Theme of Famous Last Words; UFOs: Manual for the Millennium;* and *The Hero's Journey: Joseph Campbell on His Life and Work.* He also worked with John Densmore on his best-selling autobiography, *Riders on the Storm: My Life with Jim Morrison and the Doors,* and is a contributor to twelve other books.

His screenwriting credits in documentary films, which have won more than twenty-five international awards, include *Ecological Design: Inventing the Future; The Peyote Road; The Red Road to Sobriety; The Hero's Journey: The World of Joseph Campbell;* and the 1991 Academy Award-nominated *Forever Activists: Stories from the Abraham Lincoln Brigade.*

CONARI PRESS, established in 1987, publishes books on topics ranging from psychology, spirituality, and women's history to sexuality, parenting, and personal growth. Our main goal is to publish quality books that will make a difference in people's lives—both how we feel about ourselves and how we relate to one another.

Our readers are our most important resource, and we value your input, suggestions, and ideas. We'd love to hear from you—after all, we are publishing books for you! To request our latest book catalog, or to be added to our mailing list, please contact:

CONARI PRESS
2550 Ninth Street, Suite 101
Berkeley, California 94710-2551

800-685-9595   510-649-7175
fax: 510-649-7190   e-mail: Conaripub@aol.com
http://www.readersNdex.com/conari/